Reptiles and Amphibians

John Stidworthy

Macdonald Educational

Contents

How to use this book

This book tells you about reptiles and amphibians. You will find out where they live, how they live, what they eat and how they breed. The book has been divided into two main parts. Pages 10 to 21 are all about amphibians. Pages 22 to 41 are all about reptiles. Look first at the contents page to see if the subject you are looking for is listed. For example, if you want to find out how amphibians breed, you will find that it is to be found on pages 14 and 15. The index will tell you where and how many times a particular subject is listed and if there is a picture of it. A stegosaurus, for example, is to be found on page 9. The glossary explains the more difficult terms found in this book.

Prehistoric amphibians

350 million years ago there were already small plants, insects and scorpions on the land, but there were no animals with backbones. Many kinds of fishes swam in the seas and fresh waters. Amongst these were some freshwater fish with fins which had strong muscles and bone at the base. The modern name for them is lobe-fin fish. They breathed using gills, but could also gulp air into their swim-bladders and use them as lungs. As much of the world at this time had severe dry seasons this was very useful. A lobe-fin trapped in a drying-out pool could still breathe using air. It may even have been able to wriggle from pool to pool using its strong fins as levers to help it along.

Each new generation brought minute and chance changes to these fishes' bodies. The changes were passed on to their young. Many generations and millions of years later, these fish had become what we call amphibians. Lungs became more important and gills disappeared.

Ichthyostega was one of the first amphibians. It grew to 1 metre long. It had proper limbs but still had a tail fin like a fish.

Lungfish were common 350 million years ago. Few kinds are alive today. The young are tadpole-like. Adults can breathe air. ▼

◄ Early amphibians developed from fish which looked rather like eusthenopteron. This lobe-fin may have been able to crawl over mud.

6

The bones and muscles of the fins became stronger. The fin ends developed as toes. Finally, the fins became legs to help the animals on to land.

These early amphibians were the largest land animals of their time. They survived well in and around the swamps feeding on fish, insects and other small creatures. For millions of years the amphibians ruled the edges of the land. In this time they evolved into many varieties, some quite tiny, some more than 4 metres long.

A leaky skin

Not all these amphibians lived on land. Many spent most of their time in water. Even those that lived on land were tied to water, as are most modern amphibians, for two reasons. One is that amphibian eggs must be laid in water and develop there. The other is that amphibians have never developed a really waterproof skin to stop them losing water from their bodies to the air. One group solved these problems, but once they did so they stopped being amphibians. They became what we know as reptiles.

Cyclotosaurus, over 4 metres long and the largest amphibian ever known, lived a life like a crocodile in water 200 million years ago.

Remains of branchiosaurs show that 300 million years ago, as now, amphibians passed through a larval stage with external gills. ▼

▲ 220 million years ago the first frogs like this triadobatrachus had already evolved. The frogs survived when many amphibians died out.

7

Prehistoric reptiles

The reptiles were the first backboned animals that could live on land all the time. Their dry scaly skins were waterproof and they could get right away from water and make a living where no amphibian had ever gone. Reptiles also laid eggs with shells. In these eggs the young could develop protected from the outside world, in their own private ponds, without needing to be in water. Some reptiles could also eat plants. Unlike the fish and amphibians, which only fed on other animals, some of the early reptiles developed special teeth for crushing plant food. They were doing something which had not been done before by animals with backbones.

Reptiles were more versatile than amphibians and gradually they crowded out the large amphibians which had ruled the land edges before. By 200 million years ago reptiles were the most important group of large land animals. In their long history the reptiles gradually

▲ Early reptiles, like limnoscelis, were clumsy creatures with heavy skulls and sprawling legs. This one was 1.5 metres long.

◀ The huge sail on the back of the meat-eater dimetrodon may have helped it warm itself in the sun. It did not fold down.

changed and many new types evolved. The clumsy and sprawling early reptiles gave way to kinds which could bring their legs right under their bodies, making it easier for them to support their weight and move quickly. Dinosaurs were built like this. Other reptiles took to the air. Some even returned to the water and became successful hunters in the sea. Reptiles ruled the world.

The downfall of the great reptiles

Then, about 65 million years ago, there seems to have been a sudden cooling of the climate. The large reptiles and many other animals could not cope with this and died out. The period which followed was one in which the mammals, and not the reptiles, were the largest land animals.

But the reptiles had not disappeared completely. Many smaller kinds survived, just as some small amphibians had survived the coming of the reptiles. Today amphibians and reptiles are still found in surprising numbers, living in a great variety of ways.

▲ Early kinds of pterosaur went gliding through the air on leathery wings. Pteranodon was one of the biggest, with a 9 metre wingspan.

Stegosaurus was a plant-eating dinosaur which lived about 150 million years ago. It had a small brain but strong armour.

Tyrannosaurus was one of the last dinosaurs. It was one of the biggest meat-eaters which ever lived, with teeth like daggers. ▶

Amphibian types

Adult amphibians have quite different lives from their newly-hatched young. The young usually live in water whereas most adults can also live on land. It is this dual life which makes amphibians different from the other backboned animals and also gives them their name— the word amphibian means 'two-lives'.

There are three main groups, or orders, of amphibians. The smallest group, and perhaps the oddest, are the *apodans*. These look rather like worms with grooves ringing the skin. They have no legs and live underground. They are found in tropical areas and about 170 species are known.

There are more than 300 species of what we call *urodeles*. These are the amphibians with obvious tails, such as newts and salamanders. They usually have four legs but these are often small compared with the body.

The frogs and toads

By far the biggest order of amphibians are the *anurans*, meaning 'without-tails'. There are over 2,000 species of frogs and toads. Compared with other amphibians the backbone is very short and stiff, and the back legs are well developed for jumping and kicking out when swimming.

The largest amphibians are the giant salamanders of eastern Asia, growing to 1.6 metres long, but most are small animals, ten centimetres long or less. The smallest, a tiny Cuban frog, is only 1.2 centimetres long.

How amphibians breathe

An amphibian's skin is smooth with no scales. Instead there are many mucous glands which keep the skin moist. Amphibians have rather simple balloon-like

◀ The caecilian belongs to the apodan group. Unlike other amphibians, they have tiny scales embedded in their skins.

Most newts and salamanders live in the northern hemisphere. Most are small, like this marbled newt which grows to 12 cm. ▼

lungs which are weak compared with ours. Many amphibians also breathe through their skins and mouth linings. One whole group of salamanders has no lungs and just relies on breathing through their skins.

Amphibians are most common in the tropics but some live in cool climates and on mountains. Although they like water they cannot live in the sea.

The frogs are the most successful of amphibians and are found in all the continents (except Antarctica). Salmin's frog comes from Australia. It lives underground, only emerging during rainy periods.

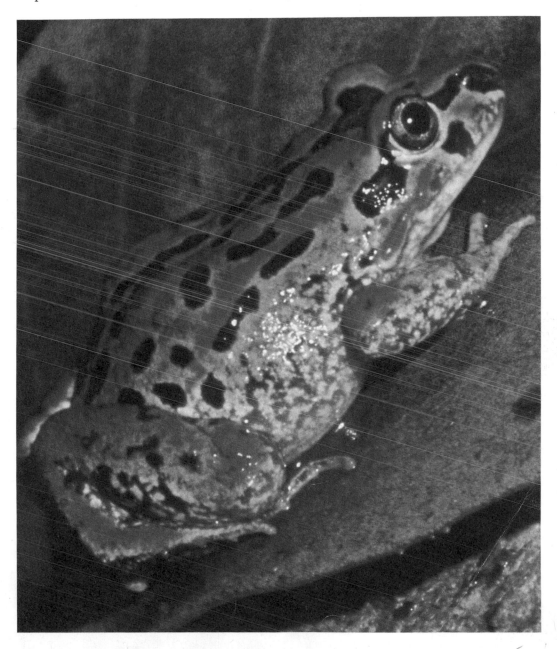

Senses and behaviour

When the amphibians moved on to the land their sense organs changed. Eyes used out of water need to be kept moist and clean on the surface. Land amphibians have eyes protected by eyelids and keep them wet with tears. The lower eyelid is moveable and can close the eye. A transparent fold makes a third eyelid which cleans the eye surface. Amphibians which live permanently in water still have fish-like eyes without eyelids. Amphibians which always live in the dark may have no eyes at all.

Bulging eyes

Many amphibians have eyes bulging from the top of the head. Even if the animal is in water this gives the eye a greater chance of being above water where it works better and can see further. The eyes are good at seeing things like an insect moving, or a large shadow looming up. These are the things the animal must notice and react to in order to survive.

◀ The male painted reed frog blows out its throat sac as it signals its presence to a possible mate. As with birds, many kinds of frogs can be identified by their voices during the breeding season. The balloon-like sac amplifies the sound.

Finding a mate

Many amphibians have bright colours and patterns which help them recognize their own kind. In newts there may be a big difference between sexes, especially in the breeding season, when some males develop large crests. Males attract females to breed by putting on a display, bending and waving their tails. Sounds are also important for some amphibians. Some find their prey partly by hearing. Often frogs and toads find their mates by hearing. Many croak or cheep when at their breeding pools. Males have the loudest voices and may have special croaking sacs in the throat to magnify the sound. The size, number and shape of these sacs vary in different species.

Hearing on land and in the water

All backboned animals have internal ears in the skull. As sound travels well through water and through animals which are in water, they have no need for ears on the outside of the body. On land it is a different story. Sounds from the air will not easily go through an animal and it must have ears on the outside to be able to hear. In frogs and toads a large eardrum can often be seen. This connects with the inner part of the ear in the skull by a bony rod. Their hearing seems quite good and is usually specially tuned to the kinds of noises made by their own species.

Sensing movement and smell

Amphibians have noses which can work well in both air and water. Their skins are sensitive to touch, warmth, and some chemicals. Tadpoles and some amphibians which spend all their lives in water have a *lateral line*. This is a special line of organs sensitive to touch, which can feel movements in the water. These organs help the animal in finding its food.

Most amphibians live solitary lives except during the mating season when they may crowd together in large numbers. Some kinds also group together when hibernating. Amphibians are not very intelligent. Some only recognize food if it moves, but they are good at finding their way back to one particular place.

▲ A male great crested newt which is in breeding condition has high spiky crests on its body and tail. The male displays by standing crossways in front of the female, bending his head towards her and vibrating it.

◀ The visible part of the frog's ear is the large eardrum at the back of its head behind the eye. The large eyes bulge from the top of the head. As the head cannot turn, this helps give all round vision.

adult frog

12 weeks

8 weeks

2 weeks

Common frogs' eggs hatch after about a week. After about 12 weeks the froglet comes on to land. The frog is adult at three years.

Breeding

In cool climates amphibians breed in early spring. They make their way to ponds where they lay their eggs. The common frog has a fairly typical life-history for an amphibian. After a short courtship, conducted by croaking, the male mounts the female, grabbing her with special pads on his thumbs. The female lays her eggs, perhaps 2,000 or more, and as she does so the male sheds his sperm and fertilizes them. Soon the familiar jelly swells round each egg to give a mass of frogspawn.

Tadpoles
Protected in the jelly, the eggs grow into tiny tadpoles which hatch and swim through the water. They breathe with external gills. These gills are soon covered up by a flap of skin. Later legs grow, the tail shrinks, the gills disappear and are replaced by lungs. Finally, the tadpole becomes a tiny frog which moves to land.

This is the 'normal' way for an amphibian to reproduce, but there are many variations. Toads, for instance, lay strings of eggs wound round plants rather than masses of floating spawn. Newts stick single eggs to plants. The male newt deposits a little packet of sperm which the female picks up and takes into her body, so the egg is fertilized before laying.

Other ways of breeding
Some amphibians lay their eggs in temporary pools. These eggs can go through their whole development very quickly before the pool dries up.

A number of amphibians carry their eggs on their own bodies. The male poison-arrow frog carries eggs attached to the skin of its back. Other frogs carry them in a special pouch, or in the case of the Surinam toad, in sixty individual pockets on the female's back.

A frothy nest

Some tree frogs lay their eggs out of water in special froth nests. The froth is beaten up by their legs from the slime around the eggs. The froth in the middle of the nest breaks down and forms a little pond for the tadpoles as they develop. When they get bigger they drop into the water below where they finish off their development.

Frogs hatched in their father's mouth

Perhaps the oddest way of looking after the young is practised by the male Darwin's frog. The female lays the eggs on damp ground. When the eggs begin to move in their jelly, the male swallows them and keeps them inside his large croaking sac. Here the eggs go through a short tadpole stage. Eventually the tiny young frogs are ready to come out. The father opens his mouth and they hop out.

Live births

Some salamanders, such as the alpine salamander, do not lay their eggs but keep them inside their bodies. The young go through their development inside the mother and are born as complete but small versions of their parents.

Many of the odd ways in which amphibians breed give protection to the young. They may need to breed in these ways because water is so scarce.

▲ A tree frog's froth nest. Later the tadpoles will fall into the water below.

The eggs of the midwife toad are looked after by the male. The eggs are wrapped round its back legs. When the eggs are ready to hatch, the male goes back to the water. ▼

Feeding and defence

The amphibians are all meat-eaters and feed on live animals. As they are mostly small animals themselves, their prey usually consists of insects, spiders, small fishes and worms. The larger frogs may feed on reptiles, small birds or mammals as large as rats. Some species eat other amphibians, sometimes even their own kind.

Two main methods of attack are used. Many simply grab their prey in the jaws and swallow. Others use their tongues. In many frogs and toads the tongue is sticky and attached only at the front of the mouth. It can be flicked out to catch the prey. A few kinds of salamanders also have tongues which they shoot out. Amphibians may have small teeth on both jaws, and sometimes on the roof of the mouth too. Others are toothless. Their prey is swallowed whole rather than chewed up.

▲ A leaf frog is hiding here!

Horned frogs can be up to 25 cm long. They have a nasty reputation and will attack almost anything moving that they can swallow, including snakes and small mammals. ▼

Camouflage against enemies

As amphibians have no large teeth, spines or claws they would seem to be rather defenceless. In fact many have a very good defence in their colouring which matches their surroundings perfectly, as in green tree frogs. Some

have another sort of camouflage which breaks up their outline so that enemies do not spot them easily. Amphibians stay still for long periods and this makes them harder to see.

Another form of defence is escape. Some frogs make huge leaps when frightened—one kind of frog can jump 36 times its own length! Many amphibians can swim surprisingly fast when alarmed.

If they cannot escape, some amphibians try to bluff their way out of trouble. Toads will puff themselves up and raise themselves up on their hind legs so that they look bigger and frighten off enemies.

Nasty tasting amphibians

Many amphibians have glands in the skin which make substances that taste nasty to other animals or are poisonous. Those which are particularly nasty are often brightly coloured in black and red, yellow or orange. These colours act as warning notices to their enemies. Sometimes, as in fire-bellied toads, the animal has a bright underside which it shows only when alarmed. Some of the brightly coloured poisonous frogs in South America are used by the natives to make poison for the tips of the arrows which they hunt with.

▲ This fire salamander is eating a baby mouse. Its colours warn off attackers. If handled roughly, it gives off a nasty tasting poison which frightens off its attacker.

A common toad trying to bluff a grass snake. ▼

▲ This Pyrennean mountain salamander, like most salamanders, leads a secretive life. Hiding beneath rocks, its colour blends well with the mud in a mountain stream.

A spadefoot toad digs using its black sharp edged pad on the inside of its foot. ▼

Life on the land

Most amphibians are limited in the way they live by two great needs, warmth and dampness. Amphibians cannot keep themselves warm and must live in places which are warm enough to keep their bodies in working order. However, a few live in surprisingly cool places. The common frog, for instance, is found within the Arctic Circle in Scandinavia. In such cool climates normal life is impossible in the winter and amphibians have to hibernate. They crawl into a hole, or mud at the bottom of a pond, and stay inactive until the spring.

Hot places and deserts

Hot dry conditions are also difficult for amphibians because they lose water

Tree frogs have large eyes and in some species they even face forward so that they can judge distances when they are jumping through the branches. Those tree frogs with webbed feet use them as parachutes rather than for swimming. This is best shown in flying frogs.

through their skins so fast. A small amphibian would soon die if exposed to hot sun in the open. It is not surprising that most amphibians are secretive animals, hiding in damp shelters and venturing out in the evening or at night.

In spite of this some manage to live in deserts. The Australian water-holding frog spends most of its life in a burrow well below the surface. It comes up only to make use of the brief rains. This is when it breeds, the young going through their development very rapidly. It also absorbs water into its body and stores a large amount in its bladder before going down to sit out another long period of drought. Some other amphibians burrow. The spade-foot toads of Europe dig themselves into sandy soil using their hind feet. Most apodans push themselves through the soil like worms.

Tree frogs that climb and fly

Quite a number of frogs are expert climbers and have taken to life in the trees. Tree frogs have extra long toes with large pads on the ends to give a suction grip. The large eyes help them see their way as they jump. Some have eyes which look mainly forwards to help them to judge distances.

Webbed feet are used as parachutes by tree frogs, and the webs are best developed in the so-called flying frog of South-East Asia. This can glide more than twelve metres from one tree to another. Many tree-living amphibians can spend their whole lives without going down to the ground. There are plenty of insects and other small animals to eat. There may even be enough water collected in leaves to breed in. Moist tropical forests make ideal living places for amphibians.

Life in the water

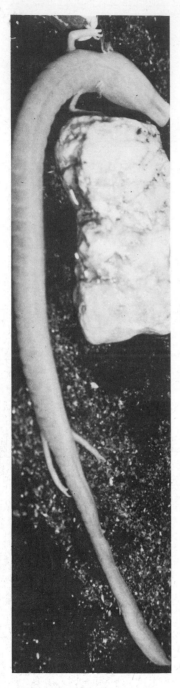

When an amphibian has changed from a *larva* into a grown adult, it is usually able to leave the water it grew up in. However, there are some adult amphibians that live permanently in water. In some ways it is an easier life. In the water they will not dry out or have to support the weight of their bodies so much. One whole family of toads, which includes the Surinam toad and African clawed toad, spend their whole lives in water. They have well developed hind legs and big webbed feet for swimming, but feeble front legs.

Sirens and giant salamanders

Several families of tailed amphibians, such as the sluggish giant salamanders, spend all their time in water. The 'congo eels' of the swamps of eastern North America are long and eel-like amphibians with tiny limbs. The sirens, of the southern states of North America, are also rather eel-like and have no back legs. They keep external gills all their lives.

Peter Pan amphibians

You would expect to find external gills in a larva rather than an adult, but some species of water-dwelling adults have them. All the *proteid* family of salamanders remain larvae in this respect and have poorly developed legs. Four of them, the mud-puppies, live in lakes and ponds in America. The most remarkable, though, is the olm of Yugoslavia. This salamander lives completely underground in caves, swimming in lakes and streams. The colourless skin makes the blood in the large gills obvious in this species. In spite of looking like larvae these salamanders can breed. The olm is unusual in that it can either lay eggs or keep them in its body to develop. It then produces a brood of two fully-formed young. The best known case of an amphibian that never really grows up is the Mexican axolotl. It belongs to a family of land salamanders but is itself a larva for life. It breeds in this state. However, if the water it is living in dries up, it can change into an adult form with lungs.

▲ Adult olms are virtually blind, but excellent swimmers. They hunt by detecting the movements of their prey in water.

The Mexican axolotl. ▶

Reptile types

There are more different living species of reptiles, over 6,000, than there are of mammals. Modern reptiles are mostly small animals. They are mainly found in the warm parts of the world. They are cold-blooded, which means they cannot produce their own body heat, and rely on warmth from their surroundings.

Reptile body processes are usually slower than ours. They can control their temperature to some extent by their behaviour, basking in the sun to warm themselves, or moving to shade to cool down. In a warm climate they maintain a fairly constant body temperature, but in a cool climate it is not so easy.

Hibernation in cold winters

Where winters are cold they hibernate, staying underground away from the danger of freezing until warmth returns in the spring. Those few reptiles which live as far north as the Arctic Circle, such as the adder and common lizard, may be inactive for the greater part of the year. In very warm places too, reptiles also rest underground in the hottest part of the year.

There are some advantages to cold-bloodedness. Less energy is required and therefore less food. It is possible for a reptile to go for a long time between meals if it uses up less energy by moving

▲ The crocodiles are amongst the largest living reptiles today. Nile crocodiles like this one can grow over 5 m long.

Fresh water tortoises are often called terrapins. They mainly eat meat; land tortoises are mainly vegetarian. This is a red-eared terrapin. ▼

very little. Some big snakes can fast for over a year with no ill effects. Large amounts of oxygen are needed only when the animals are active and are using up a lot of energy. When they are at rest for long periods, they breathe in oxygen at a much slower rate than human beings do.

Apart from being cold-blooded, laying eggs and having scales, reptiles differ from us in other ways. The circulation of blood in reptiles is not so efficient as in mammals. Blood holding oxygen comes from the reptile's lungs. When it reaches the heart, it mixes with blood from the rest of the body which contains no oxygen. This mixed blood is then returned to the body. In humans the blood does not mix in this way.

Reptiles cannot quickly break down food reserves. This fact, coupled with their poor oxygen supply, means reptiles cannot keep up any effort for long periods. Some, though, can be very active in short bursts.

New teeth for old

Reptile bones differ from ours in growing throughout life. Adult reptiles have no fixed size. Old reptiles may be giants. Most reptiles also keep growing new sets of teeth, replacing old teeth which drop out. A crocodile four metres long may have had over forty sets of teeth in its life.

There are four main groups of living reptiles. The tortoises are an ancient group, some parts of their bodies being like those of the earliest reptiles. There are still about 240 kinds of tortoises. The tuatara is the only species left in its group. This group was successful even before the time of the dinosaurs. The twenty or

more kinds of crocodile are survivors of a group which has been around for more than 100 million years. They are among the closest living relations of dinosaurs.

Lizards and snakes are relative newcomers but they are the most successful modern reptiles, with 3,000 species of lizards and nearly as many snakes. They share many features. Lizards usually have legs, though some lack them. Snakes never have fully developed legs.

This tree python becomes an emerald green when adult. Pythons are old-fashioned snakes which still have remnants of legs. ▼

Lizards are familiar animals in warm climates. They are usually small and feed on other animals. ▼

The rare tuatara is now a protected animal in New Zealand, where it lives on just a few coastal islands. ▼

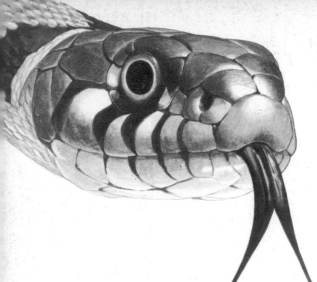

Senses and behaviour

Reptiles have, like us, several ways of finding out about their surroundings. Many have very good eyesight. Most lizards have very sharp daytime vision and can see in colour, as can tortoises. Snakes generally cannot see so well. This is not surprising as snakes probably evolved from lizards which burrowed underground and had little use for eyes.

▲ Snakes have no eyelids and cannot blink or shut their eyes to sleep. A glassy scale covers the snake's eye. The tongue is used to collect scents. There are no outer ears and a snake is deaf.

Reptile hearing

Ears do not seem very important to most reptiles. In many kinds the opening to the eardrum can be seen at the back of the head. The geckos and the crocodiles seem to have the best ears amongst reptiles. Geckos make clicks and chirps and crocodiles roar in the mating season. Most reptiles do not communicate in this way and can only hiss. A number of kinds of lizards have good hearing. A few lizards and all snakes are deaf to sounds in the air, but they may be able to feel vibrations through their bodies.

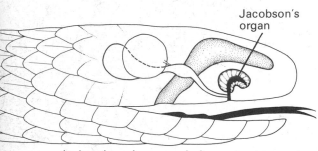

Jacobson's organ

▲ Jacobson's organ is important to many reptiles and is well developed in snakes. Like a snake's tongue, it is forked. It is sensitive to chemicals gathered by the tongue. Glands near the eye keep it moist.

An odd way to smell

Reptiles may smell with their noses, but this seems less important than the chemical sense provided by Jacobson's organ. This is in the roof of the mouth. In many reptiles the tongue gathers scent particles and carries them to the organ for 'smelling'. All snakes have this organ and are

◀ At night, when it is active, the gecko's pupils open wide, but they can close to narrow slits to avoid daytime dazzle. Some kinds have no moveable eyelids and clean their eyes by using their tongues.

Many lizards use visual signals to show their mood. The frilled lizard rears up, spreads its throat frill and opens its mouth when it thinks it may be attacked. It may also do this to threaten rivals. ▶

specially good at following trails with it.

Rattlesnakes and pythons have another sense we do not have. They have special pits on the face which can detect heat and help them find warm-blooded prey. The tuatara and some lizards have an eye-like structure under the skin at the top of the head. This seems to warn them when they have been out too long in the sun.

Reptiles of very little brains

The information coming to a reptile through its senses is received by a small brain. Even a crocodile's brain is scarcely bigger than your thumb. Other reptiles have even smaller brains. Not surprisingly, therefore, reptiles show few signs of intelligence. Most reptile behaviour consists of a small range of actions or responses to the things in the world around them.

Reptile displays

A male lizard may defend its territory and court females by bobbing its head or body. Some lizards use colours and patterns to help their displays. The reaction of another lizard depends on whether it is a rival male or a possible mate. Two female lizards usually ignore each other.

The ears of a crocodile are housed under a flap of skin behind the eye. When a crocodile is in the water it often rests so that ears, eyes, and nose are just above the surface and can be used out of water. ▶

▲ Young copperhead snakes are born live in transparent sacs. They are about 23 cm long at birth.

Young crocodiles hatching can squeak whilst still in their eggs. This attracts their mother to help them in hatching. ▼

Breeding

When reptiles mate the male places sperm inside the female. The eggs are fertilized within the female, and are then laid.

Reptile eggs may have hard shells, as in crocodiles and tortoises, or leathery parchment-like shells. The shape varies. Most reptiles lay oval eggs, but some turtles lay round eggs and a few lizards lay long thin ones. There are usually very many eggs. The highest number is laid by some sea turtles which may lay clutches of up to 200 several times in a season. Large crocodiles also lay clutches of 50 or more eggs at a time.

Mothers who abandon their young
Reptile eggs are usually left by the mother after being buried in sand, soil or vege-tation. They are kept warm by their sur-roundings. The average time it takes for most reptile eggs to hatch is 6-12 weeks, but it also depends on the outside tem-perature. The young hatch as tiny ver-sions of their parents. They must find their own food and avoid enemies. The lack of parental care explains the need for large numbers of eggs. Many eggs and young reptiles are eaten by enemies. Out of the hundreds of eggs laid by a turtle, few are likely to live to become adults and breed.

Looking after the eggs and young
A few kinds of reptiles take a little more care of their young. Crocodiles and alli-gators will sit on top of the nest. Pythons coil round their eggs. These actions help to guard the eggs. Crocodiles and a few

lizards have been seen to help their young at, or just after, hatching.

Live births for a few reptiles

Some reptiles give birth to live young rather than laying eggs. In these the egg is kept inside the mother until about to hatch. The baby is born in a soft membrane from which it breaks free. A number of snakes and lizards do this, often species which live in either very cold or hot places. The eggs get the advantage of moving around with their mother to keep at the ideal temperature.

To cut free from the egg or membrane, baby lizards and snakes have a special egg-tooth which they quickly lose. Other reptiles use a bump on the tip of the snout. A newly-hatched reptile may have enough yolk left to keep it going for weeks, but some kinds must feed within a few hours of hatching. Poisonous snakes can use their poison as soon as they are born or hatched.

▲ This sea turtle swims thousands of kilometres to lay its eggs in the night. It digs a pit about 60 cm deep and covers the eggs with sand when it has finished.

These are young blue-tongued skinks. Like most other baby reptiles, they are not looked after by their mother after birth. ▼

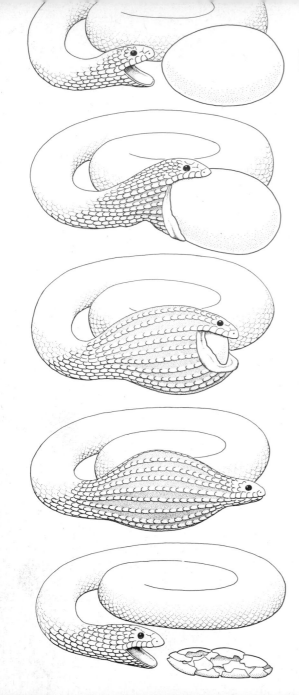

Feeding

Most modern reptiles feed on other animals, but many can only recognise their prey when it moves. Land tortoises eat mainly plant food, as do some sea turtles and a few lizards such as iguanas. Most reptiles have cone-shaped teeth all round their jaws. These are good for grabbing and holding prey, but are poor at biting off pieces to swallow and no good for chewing.

Most reptiles catch things smaller than themselves and swallow them whole. Some crocodiles may catch animals as big as antelope and cattle. They tear large food like this by shaking it or twisting it over and over in the water. Tortoises and turtles have no teeth but use instead a tough, horny beak over the jaws.

Most reptiles lie in wait or else slowly stalk their prey. When they are close enough, they rush out and grab it with their jaws. Some, like the chameleons,

◀ This African egg-eating snake only eats birds' eggs. To do this it has become very specialised. Its teeth have been reduced to small knobs which are used only to grip the egg.

The chameleon's tongue can be catapulted out in 1/16 second to its full length. Sticky saliva on the end traps an insect. $\frac{1}{4}$ second later the insect is in the chameleon's mouth. ▼

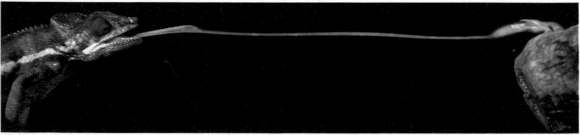

have more specialised ways of catching food.

Snakes which suffocate their prey

Constrictors include the largest kinds of snakes, such as some pythons and boas. They strike with the head and then wrap coils of their body around the prey. The victim is slowly suffocated. It is then swallowed whole, even though it may be two or three times as wide as the snake's head. This is possible because snakes have very flexible jaws and can let the bottom jaw down from the rest of the skull. Each side can work separately.

Poisonous snakes

About a third of all snakes are poisonous and use their poison to kill their prey. Vipers and cobras have special venom glands which run straight into fangs at the front of the mouth. When the snake bites, the fangs work like hypodermic syringes, injecting venom to kill their victims.

Many people think constricting snakes kill their prey by crushing them to death. This is not true. Their prey die from suffocation. This python is killing a rat.

When a viper's mouth is closed its fangs are folded flat in its mouth. When the mouth is opened to bite, the fangs fold out. Muscles squeeze poison from the gland into a hole in the tooth's root. ▼

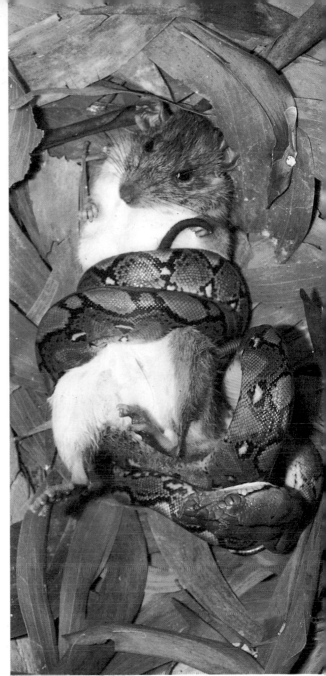

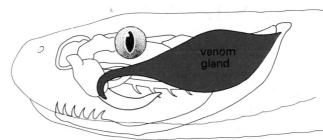

venom gland

Defence

Many reptiles are protected by armour. Lizards such as horned lizards have large spiny scales. Plated lizards and crocodiles have bony plates which reinforce the scales from below. The best developed armour of all is found in the tortoises. Instead of having scales, tortoises have a horny outer shell. Inside this is a bony box going right round the body. It consists of backbone, ribs and bony plates from the skin. All these join into one strong structure.

A bony shell to retreat into

Most tortoises can withdraw their heads and legs into their shells if attacked. Some tortoises even have shells which are hinged and work like trap doors. The tortoise can shut the door when it is not safe outside.

Many reptiles have colours and patterns which make them hard to see, especially as they can stay still for long periods. Their camouflage protects them from their enemies and hides them from their own prey.

Disposable tails

A special defence used by many lizards when attacked is to break off their tails. The lizard can shed its tail of its own accord and leave it behind to confuse its enemy. The enemy concentrates on the wriggling tail while the lizard makes its escape. Later it will grow a new tail.

▲ This puff adder's colours blend in very effectively with the dry stones in the desert where it lives.

◄ A frightened cobra stretches its hood with special ribs. This displays its special warning markings.

▲ Frightened grass snakes roll on their backs, go stiff and hang out their tongues. They are pretending to be dead.

To confuse an enemy, a lizard sheds its tail. Later a new one grows. Sometimes this goes wrong and two tails re-grow! ▼

How snakes get rid of their enemies

Some snakes distract enemies by turning on their backs and pretending to be dead. Venomous snakes can protect themselves by biting, but, besides wasting venom, this means coming dangerously close to an enemy, so some venomous snakes are brightly patterned and coloured to warn off enemies. Other snakes puff up and hiss when they feel threatened, whilst cobras have startling hoods. Rattlesnakes use the horny beads at the end of their tails to make a buzz which puts off enemies.

Some harmless snakes bluff their way out of trouble by being coloured like dangerous snakes. Others hiss, puff themselves up or make attacking movements with their heads and even tails.

Moving about

Few present-day reptiles can walk with their bodies supported above their legs. Crocodiles *can* do this, but they usually move with their legs sprawled sideways, as do other reptiles.

Reptile legs are attached to the sides of their bodies and not underneath as, for example, in horses. This means it is much harder work for reptiles to support their bodies and so they usually flop on their bellies when resting. Some drag their bodies along the ground even when moving.

Reptile legs act as levers to push on the ground. However, much of the work of walking is done by muscles along the backbone. These bend the body from side to side as the reptile moves.

Reptiles go faster on two legs

Generally, reptiles do not move quickly. A few lizards can increase their speed by running on two legs rather than four. Basilisks, bearded lizards and collared lizards can move in this way. For very short periods, the collared lizard can reach speeds of up to 25 kilometres an hour. Two-legged runners have particularly long back legs.

Some lizards increase their speed by running on two legs. They use their tails to help them balance when running. ▼

Running on the water

The basilisk lizard can even continue its two-legged run on water. Its back legs have special tiny pads to help it achieve this. If the water surface is smooth, it can carry on running for several seconds. When it can no longer run like this, it simply dives and carries on its way by swimming.

Leglessness

All snakes and some lizards are legless. There are some lizards with very well developed legs, some with very short

Worm snakes live underground and so have tiny eyes which can only tell the difference between light and dark. They have special heads and tails to help them burrow. ▼

legs, some with only two legs, and some with no legs at all. In the family of skinks, for example, different types of skinks show all these different stages of leg development.

Loss of legs is often linked to burrowing habits. Burrowers can usually wriggle through soil without using legs, just using their long bodies, although one of the champion burrowers is the gopher tortoise which can dig a burrow ten metres long with its feet.

Underground lizards

One group of lizards, the *amphisbaenians*, spend their whole lives underground. Their name means 'going both ways' and they can go forwards or backwards in their burrows. They have a worm-like appearance and almost invisible eyes.

Several kinds of snakes are also burrowers with tiny eyes. In fact, it is believed that the lack of legs in snakes, and some of their other odd features, are due to a burrowing past.

How snakes move

Most snakes move on land by the usual reptile method of bending the backbone, but as the body is very long it is bent in several waves. As there are no legs, the outside curves of the body push against the ground and push the animal along. It is usually a slow way to move and most snakes move more slowly than a man walking. The fastest go little more than ten kilometres an hour, and only in short bursts.

Snakes also move by creeping forward in a straight line by lifting and moving the belly scales. Pythons and other thick-bodied snakes move in this way.

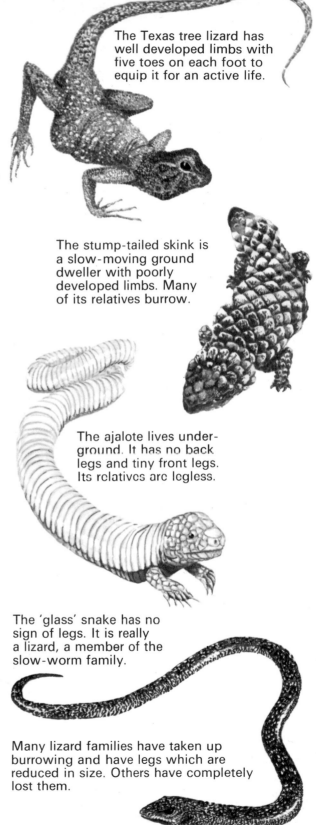

The Texas tree lizard has well developed limbs with five toes on each foot to equip it for an active life.

The stump-tailed skink is a slow-moving ground dweller with poorly developed limbs. Many of its relatives burrow.

The ajalote lives underground. It has no back legs and tiny front legs. Its relatives are legless.

The 'glass' snake has no sign of legs. It is really a lizard, a member of the slow-worm family.

Many lizard families have taken up burrowing and have legs which are reduced in size. Others have completely lost them.

Desert life

Lizards, tortoises and snakes are often seen in dry areas and deserts. In some ways reptiles are ideal animals for living in deserts. Their skins lose little water, and instead of losing water by producing waste as liquid *urine*, they produce a fairly dry paste. They therefore need very little water to replace losses. Often they get all the water they need from food or from any drops of dew which form at night. The thorny devil lizard lives in Australian deserts. It collects dew all over the outside of its body. Tiny grooves in its skin channel the water to its mouth to be drunk.

Avoiding the desert heat

Reptiles in the desert are likely to suffer from the heat. If their body temperature is too high, they die. They avoid this fate by a number of tricks. Some lizards and most snakes are *nocturnal*. They hide in rocks or underground during the day and only come out at night.

Many desert reptiles are a sandy colour. Not only is this good camouflage, but the light colour reflects more of the sun's rays than a dark colour would.

Keeping off the hot sand

Where the sand surface is very hot, a lizard may hold itself clear off the ground, making contact with the hot ground as little as possible. Postures to control body temperature are also important. In the early morning a lizard may turn its whole side or back to the sun to warm up. As the day heats up it turns so that less of its body is exposed to the sun. During the hottest part of the day the lizard finds somewhere to shelter from the blazing desert sun.

Moving on the sand

A sandy desert can be difficult to move on and therefore the palmate gecko has webbed feet which spread its weight and stop it from sinking. Many skinks manage in a different way by having smaller legs and moving through the surface sand with a swimming motion of the body. Lizards which do this have very smooth scales.

In a desert food may be scarce, or may only be available for short periods. The Gila monster stores fat in its tail in times of plenty. It retreats underground when conditions are harsh and lives from its store. The stump-tailed skink and other lizards have similar stores.

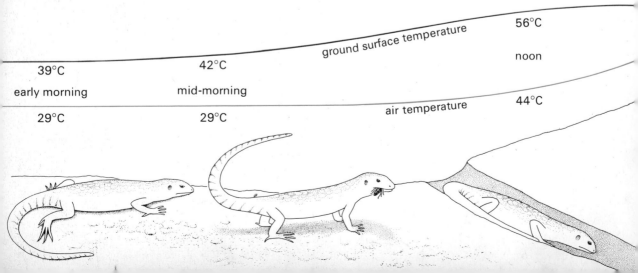

ground surface temperature

56°C

noon

39°C

42°C

early morning

mid-morning

29°C

29°C

air temperature

44°C

▲ Out of about 3,000
kinds of lizards, the Gila
monster is one of only
two that are poisonous.
Living on stored food, it
can fast for as long as
three years if there is a
drought.

The thorny devil, or
moloch, is about 15 cm
long. It eats mainly ants
and can eat up to 5,000
at one sitting. As it eats
these one at a time, a
meal may last a long
time! ▶

◀ Many reptiles control
their body temperatures
by changing their position
or the way they stand
according to conditions.
Lizards 'stilt' when they
raise themselves above
hot sand on their legs.

Life in the trees

Many lizards climb rocks or small trees with little difficulty. Relying on their lightness and their claws for gripping, they use their tails to balance with.

Some lizards, though, are specialists and spend most of their time in the trees. Chameleons are beautifully adapted for life in the trees. All four feet can grasp twigs because two toes on each foot fold in an opposite direction to the other three. The tail can curl round a twig and grasp it firmly. Their eyes are set on turrets and can swivel in any direction. When needed, both eyes can face forward and together judge the distance of an object. This is very important for seeing where to move when climbing and also for catching prey.

Feet with suction pads

Geckos are particularly good climbers. Their feet end in very sharp claws and

▲ The flying dragon lives in the forests of South-East Asia. It can leap up to 20 metres from one tree to another using its special gliding membrane. This is a flap of skin on each side of the body supported by the ribs. The 'wings' are folded down when not in use.

Kirtland's tree snake is slender and light. It is able to climb well. The snout is grooved so that the eyes have a good view forwards. The pupils are an unusual keyhole shape. Its vision is better than that of most snakes. It feeds on lizards and small birds and, although well camouflaged, has a brightly coloured tongue to lure prey close. It has a poisonous bite. ▶

◄ The flying snake is an expert climber. It also descends in a spectacular way. It spreads its ribs, flattens its body and parachutes to a lower level of the forest.

▲ Pads and projections under a gecko's toes.

▲ The parachute gecko from South-East Asia can glide through the air. It is supported by the fringe of scaly skin running along the sides of its head, body and tail. Webbed feet also help it glide. When resting, the flaps of skin help hide the gecko against a tree bark background.

◄ Most of the 80 species of chameleon live in trees and bushes. Their feet and tails are perfectly designed for gripping branches. They are also famous for their ability to change colour and camouflage themselves by matching colours with their surroundings. As they move very little and have slim bodies, they are often very hard to notice.

underneath the toes there are pads which stick to the surface the gecko is climbing. Geckos can climb trees with ease and sometimes they come into houses and walk across ceilings and even up glass. The secret is in the pads underneath the toes. From these extend microscopic fibres which have several endings, each like a tiny suction pad. There may be literally millions of these on a gecko's foot.

Tree snakes

Many snakes are also expert climbers. They usually have thin light bodies. Rough scales help them to grip branches.

A lot of snakes which live in trees are coloured so as to blend in with their backgrounds. This helps them catch unwary birds and lizards which live in the trees. One snake is so well camouflaged, that birds will sometimes mistake it for a branch and perch on it!

▲ The softshell turtle lacks horny plates on the outer shell. As well as using its snorkel nose, it breathes through its skin. Many softshell turtles are very active.

The alligator snapping turtle is one of the largest freshwater turtles and weighs up to 100 kg. It lies in the mud on river bottoms and lures fish to its jaws. ▼

Fresh water life

Fresh water provides a home for many species of reptiles. The terrapins, or fresh water tortoises, have flat, light shells and webbed toes to propel them through the water. Crocodiles also have partly webbed feet, but these are used only for steering and slow paddling.

The main push for a swimming crocodile comes from its strong muscular tail. This is swung from side to side, the flat sides driving the animal at speed. Monitor lizards and the lizards called water dragons also swim using their tails. Many species of snakes spend some time in fresh water and these use the same wave-like curving of the body for swimming as they use to get about on land.

Reptiles coming up for air

Even water reptiles breathe air and have to return to the surface to get it. Some turtles, such as the softshells, have a long snorkel nose which they can stick on the surface to breathe. This means only a small part of their bodies shows above the water. A crocodile has nostrils on top of its snout, and is unusual among reptiles in being able to close its nose off from its mouth. Flaps on the back of the roof of the mouth and tongue can seal the mouth off from the breathing tubes. This allows the crocodile to hold prey under water without flooding its lungs.

Falling asleep on the pond bottom

Reptiles can stay submerged much longer than humans, but need to breathe when active. Some terrapins, though, manage to hibernate on the bottom of ponds.

Other terrapins are able to get oxygen through pouches opening off the *cloaca*, the excretory opening. Softshell turtles can take in oxygen from water through the skin and also through the lining of the inside of the throat.

Fish for dinner

Many fresh water reptiles are specially equipped for catching fish. All crocodiles eat some fish, but the gharial, which is a specialist fish-eater, has very long thin jaws which can snap quickly in water. Softshell turtles lurk in the mud and dart out their heads to catch fish. The matamata terrapin is well disguised by its weird shape. When a fish approaches, the matamata suddenly opens its mouth and the fish is swept in with the rush of water.

The large alligator snapper turtle has a pink projection on its tongue which looks like a worm. It can be wriggled as a lure to get fish within range of capture. One of the fishing snakes has two moveable tentacles on its nose. These may also be a lure for unwary fish.

The needle-nosed crocodile grows up to 2.4 m long and lives in East Africa. Its thin jaws can be slashed quickly from side to side in the water to catch any nearby fish. ▼

Sea life and island reptiles

Two groups of reptiles spend their lives in the sea, the sea-turtles and the sea-snakes. The only other reptiles which regularly enter the sea are salt-water crocodiles and marine iguanas. The turtles have long paddle-shaped front legs to row themselves through the water. The back legs are shorter and used for steering. Their shells are light and less bony than those of land tortoises. The biggest turtle, the leathery turtle, is one of the fastest swimmers in the sea. Sea-snakes swim by the usual snake method, but many have ribbon shaped tails to aid swimming. Their large lungs may help them float.

The salt-water crocodile grows up to 6 m long. It lives around river deltas from Australia to India. ▼

Turtles lay eggs and have to return to land to do so. Green turtles may travel over 3,000 kilometres from their feeding grounds to their breeding grounds. On land sea-turtles are slow and clumsy. Sea-snakes often overcome the problem of returning to land by having their young born alive at sea, but a few kinds still return to shore to lay eggs.

Hawksbill turtles usually live in warm shallow seas. ▼

Black and yellow sea-snakes can be found hundreds of kilometres from land. Their flat sides help them to swim fast. ▼

40

Unusual island reptiles

Many islands have their own special reptiles. Madagascar was once joined to Africa but for millions of years has been cut off. It has many kinds of chameleon and gecko found nowhere else, but it is easy to see how their ancestors got there. It is not so easy to see how reptiles have reached some volcanic islands far out in oceans. For instance the Galapagos Islands are only a few million years old and were never joined to the mainland, but several kinds of reptile live there, including giant tortoises and different kinds of iguana. It seems that their ancestors must have been carried there by sea, either swimming or on floating logs.

Geckos are found on many ocean islands. They stick their eggs on tree bark and there is a good chance the eggs will float to a new home. Island animals may be free of enemies. Size may be less important than on the mainland. Island reptiles may be smaller than their mainland relatives. They may also be giants, like the Galapagos tortoises, or the largest living lizard, the Komodo dragon of Komodo Island in Indonesia.

▲ Most mainland geckos are nocturnal. These geckos from the island of Madagascar are active in daytime.

Giant Galapagos Island tortoises are the biggest tortoises in the world. One reason for their size is that few animals competed with them for food. They weigh up to 400 kg.

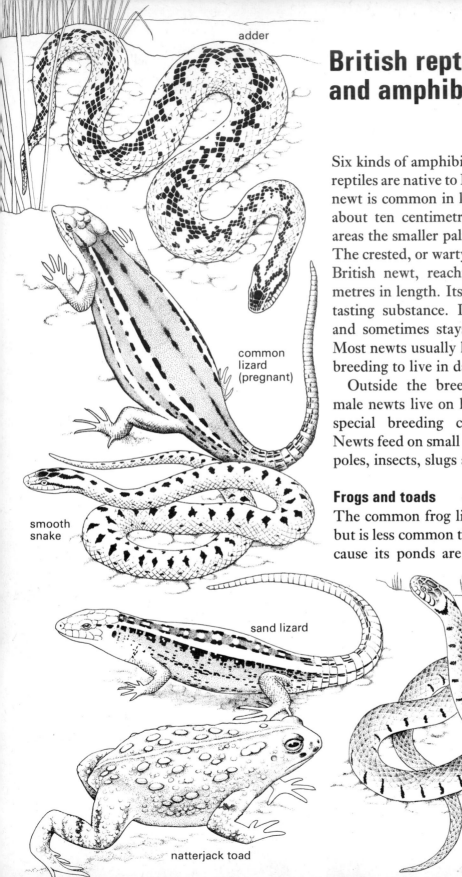

adder

common
lizard
(pregnant)

smooth
snake

sand lizard

grass
snake

natterjack toad

slow
worm

British reptiles and amphibians

Six kinds of amphibians and six kinds of reptiles are native to Britain. The smooth newt is common in lowland areas and is about ten centimetres long. In upland areas the smaller palmate newt is found. The crested, or warty, newt is the largest British newt, reaching fourteen centimetres in length. Its warts make a nasty tasting substance. It likes deep ponds and sometimes stays in water all year. Most newts usually leave the water after breeding to live in damp areas on land.

Outside the breeding season, when male newts live on land, they lack their special breeding crests and colours. Newts feed on small animals such as tadpoles, insects, slugs and worms.

Frogs and toads

The common frog lives all over Britain, but is less common than it used to be because its ponds are being filled in. Its smooth skin and hopping movement differ from the warty skin and walking movement of the common toad. The female common toad is much larger than the male.

The smaller natterjack toad is found mainly in sandy areas in south-east and north-west England. It is becoming rare as its habitat vanishes. It moves faster than the common toad and runs in short bursts.

Lizards

The common lizard is one of the hardiest British reptiles and is found all over the country. It grows as long as fifteen centimetres, half of this being tail. The rare sand lizard is a bit larger and lives in sandy areas in southern England and Lancashire. This lizard lays eggs. The common lizard has live young. Lizards eat small animals such as spiders and insects.

A legless lizard

The third British lizard is the slow worm. It has no legs but can be told from a snake by its eyelids, tiny ears and by the small scales which go across its belly. It often lives in damp places where it can burrow in surface leaf mould. It eats slugs and worms. It may break off its tail if attacked.

Harmless grass snakes

Growing up to ninety centimetres long, the grass snake is the largest British snake. It is completely harmless except to prey such as frogs and fish. Grass snakes usually live near water.

Rare smooth snakes live in sandy parts of southern England. They can reach fifty centimetres in length. They eat lizards which they kill by constriction.

Our only poisonous snake

The adder is the only poisonous snake in this country. It grows up to sixty centimetres long. The triangular head, broad body and slit-shaped pupil make it easy to recognise, even though the pattern on the body can vary quite a lot. Its bite is unlikely to kill a person, but it works quickly on small prey such as mice and lizards. Usually this is a shy snake which avoids trouble.

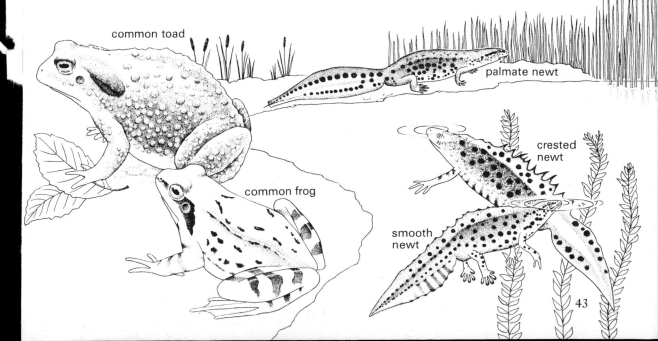

common toad

palmate newt

crested newt

common frog

smooth newt

Books to read

Reptiles and Amphibians of the World, Hans Hvass; Methuen 1978
How Reptiles and Amphibians Live, A. C. Echternacht; Elsevier/ Phaidon
The World of Amphibians and Reptiles, M. Burton; Orbis 1973
A Field Guide to Reptiles and Amphibians of Britain and Europe, E. N. Arnold and J. A. Burton; Collins 1978
The Young Specialist Looks at Reptiles, ed. A. Leutscher; Burke 1966
Living Reptiles of the World, K. P. Schmidt and R. F. Inger; Hamish Hamilton 1957
Living Amphibians of the World, D. M. Cochran; Hamish Hamilton 1961

Things to do

In Britain it is much harder to go reptile or amphibian watching than bird watching. Our amphibians are mostly secretive, and, except during the breeding season when they may flock to ponds in large numbers, they are difficult to find. You may find adults, spawn and, later, larvae of these creatures in your local pond. Unless something very bad is happening to the pond it is nearly always better to leave tadpoles to grow up there rather than try and keep them in a tank. There is a shortage of good ponds in many areas now. If you have a garden try making a pond to attract frogs and newts and help to protect them.

Reptiles are also difficult to see in Britain. Slow-worms may sometimes be found under logs or similar hiding places. Always replace logs exactly as you find them as they are important homes for many creatures. Other reptiles may be seen by keeping a sharp eye open in places where they are known to occur. On heathland, for instance, if you walk quietly and carefully, it may be possible to spot lizards or snakes basking in sheltered spots. Watch them, but do not try to touch them. You may harm them, or, if they are adders, they can harm you.

Natterjacks and smooth snakes are species protected by law and must not be captured. They should be disturbed as little as possible.

Places to go

Good collections of rare and unusual reptiles are kept by the following zoos:
London Zoo, Regent's Park, London NW1
Bristol Zoo, Clifton, Bristol
Paignton Zoological and Botanical Gardens, Totnes Road, Paignton, Devon
Twycross Zoo, Atherstone, Warwickshire
Jersey Zoological Park, Trinity, Jersey
Chester Zoological Gardens, Upton-by-Chester, Cheshire
Welsh Mountain Zoo, Colwyn Bay, Clwyd
Dudley Zoo, The Broadway, Dudley, near Birmingham
Edinburgh Zoo, Murrayfield, Edinburgh
Calderpark Zoo, Uddingston, Glasgow

Glossary

Here is a list of some of the more difficult terms used in this book.

Anuran: One of the group of amphibians with no tails—the frogs and toads.

Apodan: One of the group of amphibians with no legs, mostly living underground in the tropics.

Brood: All the offspring born to a mother at a single time.

Camouflage: Any colouring or shape which makes an animal hard to see, so that it may hide from its enemies or from its prey.

Cold-blooded: An animal that is cold-blooded is unable to keep warm by its own body processes, needing warmth from its surroundings. Fish, amphibians and reptiles are cold-blooded.

Evolve: Gradually change with time. Used for the way in which, over many generations, and thousands or millions of years, one kind of animal becomes another.

Fang: A large pointed tooth used for injecting venom.

Gills: The parts of a fish or tadpole just behind the head on each side of the body. They are used for breathing in water.

Gland: A special part of the body producing a liquid secretion such as tears or saliva.

Habitat: The kind of surroundings in which an animal is usually found and needs to live in for its particular way of life.

Hibernate: To go into a state of sleep or very low activity for the winter period, usually as a means of avoiding bad weather conditions.

Jacobson's organ: A special sense organ in the roof of the mouth which is used to detect chemicals. It is especially well developed in some reptiles.

Larva: The young stage of an animal, like a frog, after it has hatched from the egg but before it has an adult shape.

Lateral line: A line of organs along each side of a fish and some amphibians, which is well supplied with nerves. If there is a disturbance in the water the nerves send a message to the brain. The lateral line gives the animal a sense of touch at a distance.

Lung: One of the pair of sacs used for breathing air by land-living back-boned animals.

Mammal: A warm-blooded backboned animal which has hair and feeds its young on milk, such as a dog, elephant or human.

Membrane: A thin skin which has a particular job to do.

Mucous gland: A gland producing slime to keep a body surface moist.

Nocturnal: Active during the night rather than the day.

Prey: Any animal which is caught and eaten by another.

Proteid: A member of a particular family of salamanders (named after Proteus, a sea-god who could take any shape).

Pupil: The part of an eye which lets light into it. It often appears as a round dark centre to the eye.

Snorkel: A tube which can reach above the surface from under water, allowing air to be breathed.

Swimbladder: A small 'balloon' full of gas which many fish possess. It is situated in the body below the backbone. It is used by most of these fish to help keep them up in the water.

Urodele: One of the group of amphibians, such as newts, salamanders and axolotls, which generally have long tails and long bodies.

Vegetarian: Feeding on plants rather than meat.

Venom: The poison produced by some snakes. It is a special form of saliva.

Index